*N*obody ever said that it would be
easy or that the skies would always
be sunny. When gray days and worrisome
times come along, you need to stay strong.
Know that everything will be okay...
Your faith in tomorrow will <u>always</u> help
you do what is right... and it will help you
be strong along the path of life.

— *Collin McCarty*

OUR FAMOUS SAYing
to EACh Other ...
" HAng in there"....

Love,
Aunt Cameron

AlwAYS here
for You!

Hang In There

...*Life Can Be Hard Sometimes, but*
It's Going to Be Okay

A Blue Mountain Arts® Collection

Edited by Gary Morris

Blue Mountain Press™

Boulder, Colorado

Library of Congress Control Number: 2003109963
ISBN: 0-88396-755-3

ACKNOWLEDGMENTS appear on page 64.

Certain trademarks are used under license.

BLUE MOUNTAIN PRESS is registered in U.S. Patent and Trademark Office.

Printed in the United States of America.
First Printing: 2004

 This book is printed on recycled paper.
This book is printed on fine quality, laid embossed, 80 lb. paper. This paper has been specially produced to be acid free (neutral pH) and contains no groundwood or unbleached pulp. It conforms with all the requirements of the American National Standards Institute, Inc., so as to ensure that this book will last and be enjoyed by future generations.

Blue Mountain Arts, Inc.
P.O. Box 4549, Boulder, Colorado 80306

Contents

Things Are Hard Right Now, but...
Trust in Yourself
to Make a New Beginning

Sometimes life leads you
   in a new direction.
And even when you don't
   feel prepared,
or when you don't want
   to change,
you are forced to start over.
Life is like that... there are
   no guarantees.
It makes you feel scared
   or anxious or sad.

But after you've shed
   your last tear —
just when you think everything
   is out of your hands —
you take a deep breath
   and finally realize that
you have complete control.

Survival is about reclaiming
   your "self."
It is about learning to love
   who you are.

Survival is about making wise choices,
  setting goals,
and finding out what really
  makes you happy.
It is about rediscovering
  those things you always
  wanted to do.
Happiness is something that
  has to come from within.
Nobody can provide it for you.

You are a beautiful, caring,
wonderful person.
You are worthy of all good things.
Life is hard right now,
but please know that a lot
  of people are there for you…

And look on this as your new beginning!

— *Claudia McCants*

Hang In There, Hold On, and
Keep Your Spirits Up!

*I*f you ever need some extra encouragement ✦
If you would like to be reminded once in a
while that you're so special ✦ I want you to
remember this… and I hope it brings you a
smile ✦ Never forget what a treasure you are ✦
Try to realize how important you are in the eyes
of my world ✦ No matter where you go, my
hopes and my heart travel beside you every step
of the way ✦ And I know, even though difficulties
come to everyone, it isn't fair when they hang
around longer than they should ✦ If I could wish
the clouds away, the welcoming breeze of a brand
new day would warm your life right this very
minute ✦ But until a new day comes along, I
know that you'll always be strong enough to
see things through ✦

*I have so much faith in you ➤ I know how
much strength and courage you have inside ➤
I know you can find all the patience it takes ➤
You can turn to the times in the past when
challenges were met, when you survived, when
you were rewarded with success, and when you
learned to believe in so much within you ➤
You have so much going for you, and I know
that you're going to see your way through
anything that comes along ➤ I know that
brighter days are going to find a way to shine
in your windows and chase away any blues ➤
And of all the things I am most certain of...
I know that no one deserves more smiles,
success, friendship, or love
　　...than the special person I see
　　　every time I look at you ➤*

— Brian Gill

If Ever You Need Me,
I Hope You'll Let Me Know

No one ever said life would be easy, and it seems so unfair sometimes. Yet life's ups and downs make us better and stronger, even though we may not realize it at the moment.

Remember — when you hurt, let the pain out. When you're sad, let the tears flow. When you're angry, release it. When frustration sets in, work it out. Help yourself as much as you can. You can be your own best friend.

But when you need to share your confusion, let me know. I try to know when to be there, but I can't always unless you let me know.

Love is the greatest gift we can give to one another, and giving is one of the greatest joys life bestows upon us.

I'm here to give to you, whenever and for always.

— Laurie Giglio

A Little Morale Booster

You're really something, do you know that? And in spite of whatever may happen in your day, you are going to stay that way: trying and giving and living life in the best way you know how. So keep your spirits up, and keep things in perspective. It's going to be okay.

You've made it through difficult things before, right? Right. And you always land on your feet. Maybe not dancing; maybe not always sure about what to do next. But you always manage to figure things out. Especially when you're able to keep your sense of humor and not lose your smile.

If you really thing about it, you'll realize that you are a very strong individual. Someone who may not have all the answers, but who is at least willing to hope and try and believe. You can see your way through just about _anything_; it all depends on how you look at it. And when I look at you, I see someone who really is… pretty amazing.

— Ceal Carson

Life Will Get Better!

*Hang in there and have patience
with yourself and the situation.
Live in the moment, one day at a time,
not fretting about the past
or worrying about the future.
You have strength enough for the present,
and that is all you need for now.
Allow yourself the luxury of peace,
and don't take on more than you have to.
Learn to let go.
Refuse negative thoughts;
replace them with positive ones.
Look for the good things in your life
and make a point of appreciating them.*

*Believe in yourself and know
that you have the power.
You are ultimately the one
in charge of your life
and the only person in the world
who can change it.
No matter how much others
are pulling for you
or how much anyone else cares,
you must do what needs to be done
to make your present and future
everything you want
and need it to be.
You can do it!*

— *Barbara Cage*

This Too Shall Pass

When the only thing
we can see is rain,
sometimes it's hard to believe
the storm will ever end.
But the clouds will move on
and the sun will shine bright again.

Just because we can't see a solution
does not mean there is no solution.
Trust that things will work out
as they are meant to be.
They will.
Know that I feel for you
and I would do anything
to make the sun shine warm
on your life again.

Until the rain passes,
know that you have a safe place
to share what's in your heart
and a shelter where you will be loved.

— Jason Blume

Tomorrow Is a New Day

Sometimes we do not feel
    like we want to feel
Sometimes we do not achieve
    what we want to achieve
Sometimes things that happen
    do not make sense
Sometimes life leads us in directions
    that are
beyond our control
It is at these times, most of all
that we need someone
who will quietly understand us
and be there to support us
I want you to know
that I am here for you
in every way
and remember that though
things may be difficult now
tomorrow is a new day

— Susan Polis Schutz

When Things Are Hard, Remember...
The Best Is Yet to Be

Sometimes when things are at their worst, in the long run, it can all work out for the better.

This can be a time for reflection, to look at where you came from and to visualize where you might go from here.

The hardest times can be blessings in disguise.

Often it's those times when one opportunity falls through that you are led to a better one.

*If you believe in something
strongly enough, with faith and
perseverance, you will succeed.*

*If the desire is there, you can
make what you thought was a
dream into a reality.*

*This time may seem scary,
but it's also a brand-new
beginning in your life, a new
chance for new things.*

*I know you will be all right,
and eventually you will get
what you want.*

*You can do anything once
you decide on something.*

— Carol Howard

Every Life Has
Its Ups and Downs

L *ife will always have disappointments*
and heartaches.
It never stays happy, and just as important,
it never stays sad.
Anger has its place, too,
yet it should be controlled and let go.
Happiness is almost always a state of mind
and an attitude that can be controlled
in most situations.

Choose happiness when at all possible.
Keep good memories and discard hurts
and failures.
Allow yourself to make mistakes
and realize that's when you may learn
your biggest lessons.

You are a precious and valued person
who deserves all the best in life —
take it and share it with others.

— Barbara Cage

When One Door Closes, Another One Opens

The past is an anchor
that holds us down.
Until we let go of who we were,
we can't become
who we were always meant to be.

It's hard to trust
when we don't know
what the results will be.

Believe in your heart
that there are wonderful opportunities
waiting for you —
roads waiting to be traveled
and new paths waiting to be explored.

Treat this next chapter in your life
as an adventure,
and you'll find challenges and rewards
better than any that you can imagine.

I know this is not an easy time for you.
I feel for you,
but I know things
will work out for the best.

— Jason Blume

Have Faith in Where You're Headed

Sometimes it's hard to imagine why
life throws us a curve in the road that
suddenly changes everything from what we had
imagined it would be. While there are no maps to
steer us through this rough terrain, there are certain
assurances to help guide our way.

Having faith, perhaps, is the greatest assurance of all —
faith not only in the strange workings of the universe,
but in yourself. Have faith that you are strong, capable,
deserving, and wise. Have faith that roadblocks are often
steppingstones in clever disguise, and that you're exactly
where you're meant to be — no matter how difficult it
may be to believe at any given moment.

Have faith that life is a series of lessons. There are
messages to help you understand the meaning of life
if you work long and hard enough to receive them.
Have faith that however painful it may seem at times,
you are uncovering truths of immeasurable worth.

Most of all, have faith that you are headed in the right
direction — and that at the end of every storm, you will
find waiting for you purpose, meaning, answers, and light.

— Lynn Barnhart

Your Path Will Grow Clear
If You Continue on with Hope

*It's not always easy
to have a clear sense
of who you are,
where you're going,
or what you want from this life.
To be that kind of person,
you have to prepare
and practice and work hard,
no matter what.*

*Don't be afraid to challenge
those who are bigger than you,
maybe even better than you —
because every time you do
you'll keep getting better
and growing stronger.
Little by little, the path will grow clearer,
and in time you'll look and see that
who you are, where you're going,
and what you want from this life
are the things your spirit reveals to you…
through the choices you make
and the things you do,
through your responses to the world
around you.*

— Diane Solis

Just Do Your Best, and Everything Will Be All Right

*I*t's not always easy to know
which path to follow, which
decision to make, or what to do.

*Life is a series of new horizons,
new hopes, new days, and changes
that come to you. And we all need
some help with these things from
time to time.*

*Remember these things: Dream it.
Do it. And discover how special you are.
Be positive, for your attitude will affect
the outcome of many things. Ask for help
when you need it; seek the wisdom the
world has and hold on to it. Make some
progress every single day. Begin. Believe.
And become.*

*Give yourself all the credit you're due;
don't shortchange your qualities, your
abilities, or any of the things that are
so unique about you. Remember how
precious life can be. Imagine. Invest the
time it takes to reach out for your
dreams; it will bring you happiness that
no money on earth can buy. Don't be
afraid; no mountain is too big to climb
if you do it at your own pace.*

*What's the best thing to do? That's simple:
    Do your best.
And everything else will fall into place.*

— Collin McCarty

Have Confidence in Yourself

There are a great many men and women whose strengths were only revealed to them during their darkest hours. Had they not faced these challenges, they never would have recognized their potential.

Everyone who ever lived has made mistakes. When you make mistakes, at least you're making <u>something</u>! And that's always better than nothing — even if the results don't always come out as you had hoped.

You are a complete, wonderful, and amazing work of nature. You are blessed with life. You are privileged with the ability to make decisions and act on them.

You can rarely change what happened five minutes ago — it's already in the past. However, you can change how you act five minutes from now — and for the rest of your life. <u>You</u> have the power.

— Robin Marshall

Let Your Heart Shine

You're going through a difficult time right now;
   things have happened that you never expected.
But when you step forward into the unknown,
      as you are doing now,
you discover beautiful things in your heart —
little miracles and small joys.
Sometimes out of your darkest moments
comes your brightest possibility.
In the sudden storm, you may find a rainbow.
Somehow, the wrong road will lead you
      to the right place;
you'll turn a corner, and joy will come from
an unexpected bend in the road.
In the difficult times, you rediscover
      your own resilient spirit;
you find a strong place inside you
      you never knew was there.
Sometimes when you step off a cliff,
you discover you can fly.
You learn that if you had not cried
      all those tears,
you might never have grown
      your own beautiful flowers.
Sometimes, in your darkest hour…
      you see that you can shine.

— Vickie M. Worsham

Through the Hard Times…

Sometimes, we are overwhelmed
with the obstacles
we are given in our lives,
and we ask "Why me?"
And often, when the answers elude us,
we believe that the trials
through which we suffer
are unfair and harsh.
But there <u>are</u> answers,
even though we may not recognize them.
In this world, we are all connected,
and there is a reason for whatever happens.
We must remain strong in the face of adversity
and meet the challenges one day at a time.

And as time heals us, both body and soul,
we may come to understand the meaning
    of our trials
or recognize the good that came from them.
We may take pride in knowing that we
    made it through them,
and as a result are much stronger
than we were before.

You are now going through
a difficult time in your life.
Accept that it has happened,
and know that things
    will get better.

— Judith Mammay

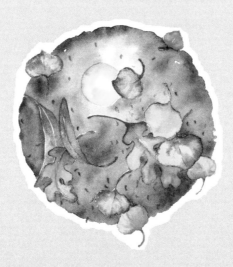

Don't Worry...
Just Keep Hoping
and Dreaming

*L*ife doesn't always follow
 the path we would like.
Sometimes, there are twists and turns.
There are small obstacles and large ones,
all of which can be overcome.

Life is a combination of tribulations
 and treasures.
Each event brings a lesson.
Don't get discouraged
 by problems that arise.
Sooner than you think,
 they will be solved.
It isn't the end of the world
 or your path.
Keep hoping and dreaming!

     — April Aragam

You Can Overcome
Any Problems That Life Has to Offer

I know that lately you
have been having problems
and I just want you to know
that you can rely on me
    for anything
you might need
But more important
keep in mind at all times
that you are very capable
of dealing with any complications
that life has to offer
So
do whatever you must
feel whatever you must
and keep in mind at all times
that we all
grow wiser and
become more sensitive and
are able to enjoy life more
after we go through
hard times

— Susan Polis Schutz

Sunny Thoughts
for a
Rainy Day

When there's a storm, don't be afraid. The sky and the elements are just doing what they do. They mean no harm.

Likewise, the challenges and unpleasantries that sometimes occur in life are there to nourish the soil of your heart and soul on your own terms. Learn from the changes. Then when the clouds clear, if there's no sign of a rainbow, go make one.

*When you can't hear the song in your
heart, maybe it's a sign you're too busy
and need to slow down. It's important to
be in touch with this melody in your life,
for it allows you to find something
positive in every reality that faces you.*

*If you can't change the circumstances,
you can at least change the way you're
looking at them. And if there's no sign
of hope, try going outside and listening
to a bird sing and imagining what it
says just before it takes flight.*

*Always be positive. Don't allow yourself
to stop trying. There's always hope, and
things will be different tomorrow. The
one thing that is constant is change.
When the night never seems to end,
know that tomorrow will come. Time
heals. Life goes on. That's just the way
it is. When you're not happy with yourself,
smile anyway. When there's no sunshine
in your life, make your own.*

— *Donna Fargo*

May This Be
a Turning Point
in Your Life

*E*ach day opens like a door,
inviting us in to the wonders of life.
Step boldly over the threshold
into the warmth
of a welcoming dawn.
Come just the way you are —
the welcome is the same
no matter who you are.
Bring a curious mind, an open heart,
and a receiving soul.
Let the wonders of life fill your spirit
to the brim.
Day after day, life flows endlessly onward,
Searching for vessels to contain its blessings.
Sometimes we do not hear the knock
at the door of dawn.
Sometimes we are too busy to accept
the invitation.
But the offer still stands,
for life must go on.

Don't miss the opportunities of each day.
Life calls you.
You have been given the desires in your heart
    so that you may answer the call to life.
There is no need to regret the wasted moments
    of the past —
no need to be down on yourself.
Each moment is a new beginning.
Start now — a new day dawns the moment
    you are ready to accept the challenges
        presented to you.
Let nothing keep you from growing into the person
    you wish to be.
Do not take yourself for granted.
You are at the right place to make a change.
May this moment be a turning point in your life.
Others may point the way to the door,
    but you must be the one to cross the threshold.
You have much to offer.
May there be many beginnings in your life.

— *Tanya P. Shubin*

Keep Soaring!

*L*ife is not always easy;
   it's not always fair, either.
It often gets our hopes up
only to let us down;
it knows how to keep us
   waiting, too,
testing both our patience
   and our faith.

I know that recently life
has left you questioning yourself
and the decisions you've made.
Just remember it's the long run
   that counts.
Though life appears to be
   one big struggle for now,
there are wonderful things
   waiting for you down the road.

If you keep trying hard
*   and wait long enough,*
these wonderful things will
*   fall in your lap.*
It's important for you to know
that I believe in you
much more than I believe
*   in many others.*
I have a good feeling about
*   your future…*
for experience has taught me
that great things come
*   to people like you*
who have the courage
*   to let their talents soar.*

— Kari Kampakis

Keep Believing

I know you have a dream in your heart. I've seen it glimmering and shining through your doubts and fears. Don't worry; we all have those moments of hesitation and uncertainty. But I want you to know — and truly believe — what a wonderful, capable person you are. I see it in the way you treat others and the amazing things you've already accomplished.

Just keep pushing forward with your plans and hopes for the future. Your life holds unlimited possibilities. Only you can know what your dreams are, and only you can make them come true. With a little faith and confidence in yourself, your talents, and your potential, you are bound to find yourself on the road to success... a beautiful path that will lead you to your dreams!

— Jane Andrews

You Have the Power to Make Your Life Everything You Want It to Be

This life is yours
Take the power
to choose what you want to do
and do it well
Take the power
to love what you want in life
and love it honestly
Take the power
to walk in the forest
and be a part of nature
Take the power
to control your own life
No one else can do it for you
Nothing is too good for you
You deserve the best
Take the power
to make your life
healthy
exciting
worthwhile
and very happy

— *Susan Polis Schutz*

Don't Avoid Life's Curveballs; Swing at Them!

*T*hings are not always easy. Life has its share of unpredictables — throwing us into situations that we're not always prepared for, expecting more from us than we're able to manage, pushing us to our limits. The adversities can be quite overwhelming, leaving us often confused and disillusioned.

Yet, it's these challenges, these tests of fortitude, that keep us going, because the payback is great when we refuse to give in. By not giving in, we discover our own internal strengths, realize our self-worth, and connect to our spiritual selves.

We find that we're made of more than we thought, and that amidst the complexities of life, we can still strive to better ourselves and beat the odds.

Life is entirely about perception — our attitudes and how we choose to act upon our intentions.

So when life throws us a curveball, instead of worrying that we aren't ready for it or that it's unexpected, we should see the moment as something to learn from and as something to incite us to grow. Most of all, we should see it as an opportunity to broaden our awareness of authentic happiness... the happiness that comes from seeing life in a whole new way.

— *Debbie Burton-Peddle*

Sometimes, It's Best to Let Go and Begin Again

There comes a time in your life when you must examine the things you have cherished so long.

There is no need to keep worn-out ideas or excess baggage. See what works for you; put aside the things that don't fit you anymore. Keep only the things that are as natural as your breath and as warm as a smile. Keep the goodness of life flowing through your heart.

The treasures in your heart are yours alone; you can do whatever you want with them.

Hope will give you more to dream about.
Trust will give you confidence. Dreams
will motivate you to excel.

Always remember that the hidden matters
of the heart are the best parts of you. Dust
them off — they are meant to be used. You
have potential within you.

It may surprise you to know how much
you have to give the world. Use the little
experiences, like grains of sand, to make
a pearl of your life. Believe that you'll
experience as much love as you give. In
expressing your highest virtues, you
become the person you were meant to
be. So look at yourself in a different way
and renew your dreams today.

— Tanya P. Shubin

When Life Gets You Down...

If the sun refuses to come out tomorrow and the rain falls too much to bring rainbows to your sky, please know that I am here with my heart wide open, a shoulder to lean on, and a great big umbrella to help keep you dry

I wish you brighter days and the strength to get through the ones filled with clouds. I wish you happiness with each day's beginning and nights filled with beautiful dreams. Know that I am thinking of you and wishing you well and that I am here if you need anything at all.

— Elle Mastro

Someone Cares
and Has Faith in You

I know that you're feeling
a little discouraged and
depressed right now, but please
remember there is someone
who cares and has faith in you.

*Remember that there's someone
who's seen you rise to the occasion
so many times; someone who knows
you've come through tough times
before and has confidence that
you'll come through this time, too.*

*Remember there is someone who
admires you, cares when you're feeling
blue, and wants you to know that
if there's any way to help, they'd be
happy to.*

*...And always remember
that someone is ME.*

— Linda Mooneyham

Be Proud of Who You Are and All You Can Be

*B*e proud of your good character. Let your actions speak loudly about your ethics. Never accept anything that goes against your conscience. Be a master gardener and let your talents blossom. Pursue the things you have a passion for. Strive to be your finest self, and not an imitation of anyone else.

Catch your dreams and make them happen. Be wise enough to ignore the people who laugh at your plans, and be sure to thank the people who support you. Always appreciate your fans.

Don't be distracted by short-term pleasures, even when you feel too exhausted to go on. It often works out for the best to take the long road, where postponed rewards lead to meaningful opportunities that touch your heart and soul.

Be an adventurer. Stake out the new frontier instead of clinging to the old and familiar. Let your pioneer spirit keep you moving forward. Visit new territories, learn new skills, and meet new people. Learn to be resilient — it will enrich you as a human being.

Don't be afraid to ask for help. Be there, as well, for someone who needs your assistance. Your heart will be glad you reached out. Keep your connections with the family you love, the friends who stand by you, and all the others who touch your life with happiness. You can never get so successful that you don't need the people who have always believed in you... and who always will.

Keep the faith that sustains you in the darkest times. With all your heart, believe you can make each day something special and every person you touch feel especially loved. Be proud of your talents and accomplishments. Speak out on your bright ideas, keep your deep concern for others, and continue on with your positive activities that bring so much goodness to this world.

— Jacqueline Schiff

You Are Not Alone

You do not always have to
play the hero
or achieve perfection
to be admired and loved.

You do not always have to be
the eternal role model
    or the strong one
who bears responsibility
    without complaint.
You do these things well
and have won the respect
    and admiration
of countless people.

But even heroes need support,
and I am here to encourage you
when doubts overwhelm you;
to be your cheerleader
when your strength wanes.
I want you to enjoy life
    without stress,
and I am here for you
    in whatever capacity you need.
You are not alone.

— Keisha McDonnough

What Lies Within Us...

*W*hat lies within us is the ability to make triumphs out of losses.

What lies within us is the ability to view things from all angles before making any final decision, as a means of determining or shaping a personal life perspective.

What lies within us is the choice of returning kindness in response to uninformed slights, and to right certain wrongs through understanding, and to be open to the changes that the quickness of life brings.

What lies within us is courage, strength, and the brilliance of shared individualities.

What lies within us is the ability to find teachers in the strangest of places, and to be teachers to those who need something that we've got... something that we didn't even know we had.

— Ashley Rice

For Those Times
When You Need Encouragement

*I*f ever you feel like giving up, don't. If you
think you can't do something, try. If you
try and fail, then try again. If you don't, you
may always wonder why you gave up so easily.

Don't let life pass you by; the only way to get
ahead is to hold your head up high. Try
not to be discouraged when things get in your
way; just climb each mountain inch by inch,
and take life day by day.

Eventually you will find the strength you had
to seek, not only to scale that mountain but
reach its mighty peak.

Believe in whatever you think is worth
believing in, and never stop until you feel you
have done all that you can to secure your
dreams… You are capable of achieving
anything you want. Always remember that.

— *T. L. Nash*

Look at It This Way…
It's Just Another
Mountain to Climb

You've faced mountains before.
Don't be afraid. You're strong.
Stare it in its face.
Get over one hurdle at a time.

You've climbed mountains before,
and this is just one more.
Keep on keeping on;
take it one day at a time.
You have what it takes.
You have your spirit, mind, and body
and the wisdom to know how to compensate.

Cry if you want. That's okay.
Kick and scream. That's okay, too.
And after you get all that out of your system,
put your worries in your suitcase
and check them at the gate so you can
lighten the load and start climbing.

Remember… it's just another mountain.
You've climbed mountains before,
and you will climb this one.
You can do it. Absolutely!

— Donna Fargo

Your Dreams Can Come True If...

Dreams can come true
if you take the time to
think about what you want in life...
Get to know yourself
Find out who you are
Choose your goals carefully
Be honest with yourself
But don't think about yourself so much
that you analyze every word and action
Don't become preoccupied with yourself
Find many interests and pursue them
Find out what is important to you
Find out what you are good at
Don't be afraid to make mistakes
Work hard to achieve successes
When things are not going right
don't give up — just try harder
Find courage inside of you to remain strong

Give yourself freedom to try out new things
Don't be so set in your ways that you can't grow
Always act in an ethical way
Laugh and have a good time
Form relationships with people you respect
Treat others as you want them to treat you
Be honest with people
Accept the truth
Speak the truth
Open yourself up to love
Don't be afraid to love
Remain close to your family
Take part in the beauty of nature
Be appreciative of all that you have
Help those less fortunate than you
Try to make other lives happy
Work towards peace in the world
Live life to the fullest

Dreams can come true
and I hope that all your dreams
become a reality

— *Susan Polis Schutz*

May You Remember This…

May today and every day of your life bring you fresh hopes for tomorrow — because hope gives all of us our reason for trying.

May each new day bring a feeling of excitement, joy, and a wonderful sense of expectation. Expect the best, and you'll get it.

May you find peace in simple things, because those are the ones that will always be there.

May you remember the good times and forget the sorrow and pain, for the good times will remind you of how special your life has been.

May you always feel secure and loved, and know you are the best.

May you experience all the good things in life —
the happiness of realizing your dreams, the joy
of feeling worthwhile, and the satisfaction of
knowing you've succeeded.

May you find warmth in others, expressions
of love and kindness, smiles that encourage you,
and friends who are loyal and honest.

May you realize the importance of patience
and accept others for what they are. With
understanding and love, you'll find the good in
every heart.

May you have faith in others and the ability
to be vulnerable. Open your heart and really share
the miracle of love and intimacy.
  Above all, may you be happy with yourself.

— Regina Hill

Always Hope for the Best

*Don't let go of hope.
Hope gives you the strength
to keep going
when you feel like giving up.
Don't ever quit believing in yourself.
As long as you believe you can,
you will have a reason for trying.
Don't let anyone hold your happiness
in their hands;
hold it in yours,
so it will always be within your reach.
Don't measure success or failure
by material wealth,
but by how you feel;
our feelings determine
the richness of our lives.
Don't let bad moments overcome you;
be patient, and they will pass.
Don't hesitate to reach out for help;
we all need it from time to time.
Don't run away from love
    but toward love,
because it is our deepest joy.
Don't wait for what you want
to come to you.
Go after it with all that you are,
knowing that life will meet you halfway.*

Don't feel like you've lost
when plans and dreams fall short
 of your hopes.
Anytime you learn something new
about yourself or about life,
you have progressed.
Don't do anything that takes away
from your self-respect.
Feeling good about yourself
is essential to feeling good about life.
Don't ever forget how to laugh
or be too proud to cry.
It is by doing both
that we live life to its fullest.

— *Nancye Sims*

Live One Day at a Time

We cannot change the past;
we just need to keep
the good memories
and acquire wisdom
from the mistakes we've made.
We cannot predict the future;
we just need to hope and pray
for the best and what is right,
and believe that's how it will be.
We can live a day at a time,
enjoying the present
and always seeking to become
a more loving and better person.

— Karen Berry

Believe in Yourself
and in Your Dreams

*I*n the pursuit of any dream,
   there will be moments
when it seems that
the dream is lost.
It is then that you must have faith
in the person that you are.
Believe that you have
the ability to overcome
any obstacle standing in your way,
and when your dream comes true,
you will realize then
what a stronger person
you have become.

— Lynn Brown

How to Stay Strong Through All of Life's Changes

*L*ife is hard. There is no way around that. It sometimes hands us things we don't really deserve, things we can't possibly understand. But despite how much our hearts are hurting, we have to find a way to believe that sometimes we're not supposed to understand. We just need to accept the circumstances and lean on the people who love us most.

It's okay to feel sad and angry and confused and a zillion other emotions that you're probably feeling right now. No one expects you to be invincible, and no one expects you to handle this completely on your own.

Lean on others and let them take care of you; that's what friends and family are for. Take each day one step at a time, and little by little those steps will get easier.

It's hard to imagine right now, that things will ever get back to normal. And they may never be exactly the same, but change is a huge part of life and of growth. It is accepting those changes that is not an easy task.

And so, more than anything right now, believe that life will get better because you are a strong and incredible person, and so many others are here to help you along the way.

— Elle Mastro

Happiness Is Waiting for You

They say that into each life some rain must fall, and we all know it's true. But there is reassurance to be found in the rainbows that follow... and in the wonder of people like you...

Nobody ever said that it would be easy, or that the skies would always be sunny. When gray days and worrisome times come along, you need to stay strong. Know that everything will be okay.

When life has got you down, remember: it's <u>okay</u> to feel vulnerable. You feel things deeply, and that is a wonderful quality to have. Rest assured that, in the long run, the good days will <u>far</u> outnumber the bad.

What is sometimes perceived as weakness is actually strength. The more you're bothered by something that's wrong, the more you're empowered to make things right. Each day is like a room you spend time in before you move on to the next. And in each room — filled with possibilities — there is a door which leads to more serenity in life.

Leave behind any little worries. Tomorrow they won't matter, and next month you may not even remember what they were. Take the others <u>one</u> <u>at</u> <u>a</u> <u>time</u>, and you'll be amazed at how your difficulties manage to become easier.

Find your smile. Warm yourself with your quiet determination and your knowledge of brighter days ahead. Do the things that need to be done. Say the words that need to be said.

Happiness is waiting for you. Believe in your ability. Cross your bridges. Listen to your heart. Your faith in tomorrow will <u>always</u> help you do what is right… and it will help you be strong along the path of life.

— *Collin McCarty*

Don't Give Up!

You're a wonderful person. Just remember
you don't have to expect so much from yourself.
Try pampering yourself a little more.
Take more time just for you, and take people up
    on their offers of help.
Try concentrating on taking just one step
and one situation at a time.
Don't try to think about everything at once.
Try putting your own best interests first,
and make time to take good care of yourself.
You are precious and important,
and you deserve peace and happiness.
It will happen if you can just hang in there.

— Barbara Cage

It's Going to Be Okay...
Just Hang in There

*I*t's going to be okay.
   Just give things a little time.
And in the meantime...
      keep believing in yourself;
      take the best of care;
      try to put things in perspective;
      remember what's most important;
      don't forget that someone cares;
      search for the positive side;
      learn the lessons to be learned;
      and find your way through to
      the inner qualities:
         the strength, the smiles,
         the wisdom, and the
         optimistic outlook
      that are such special parts
         of you.

It's going to be okay.

— *Barin Taylor*

ACKNOWLEDGMENTS

We gratefully acknowledge the permission granted by the following authors, publishers, and authors' representatives to reprint poems or excerpts from their publications.

Jason Blume for "This Too Shall Pass," and " When One Door Closes, Another One Opens." Copyright © 2004 by Jason Blume. All rights reserved.

Carol Howard for "When Things Are Hard, Remember…" Copyright © 2004 by Carol Howard. All rights reserved.

Lynn Barnhart for "Have Faith in Where You're Headed." Copyright © 2004 by Lynn Barnhart. All rights reserved.

Diane Solis for "Your Path Will Grow Clear If You Continue on with Hope." Copyright © 2004 by Diane Solis. All rights reserved.

Robin Marshall for "Have Confidence in Yourself." Copyright © 2004 by Robin Marshall. All rights reserved.

Vickie M. Worsham for "Let Your Heart Shine." Copyright © 2004 by Vickie M. Worsham. All rights reserved.

April Aragam for "Don't Worry… Just Keep Hoping and Dreaming." Copyright © 2004 by April Aragam. All rights reserved.

PrimaDonna Entertainment Corp. for "Sunny Thoughts for a Rainy Day" and "Look at It This Way…" by Donna Fargo. Copyright © 2004 by PrimaDonna Entertainment Corp. All rights reserved.

Tanya P. Shubin for "May This Be a Turning Point in Your Life" and "Sometimes, It's Best to Let Go and Begin Again." Copyright © 2004 by Tanya P. Shubin. All rights reserved.

Kari Kampakis for "Keep Soaring!" Copyright © 2004 by Kari Kampakis. All rights reserved.

Debbie Burton-Peddle for "Don't Avoid Life's Curveballs; Swing at Them!" Copyright © 2004 by Debbie Burton-Peddle. All rights reserved.

Linda Mooneyham for "Someone Cares and Has Faith in You." Copyright © 2004 by Linda Mooneyham. All rights reserved.

Jacqueline Schiff for "Be Proud of Who You Are and All You Can Be." Copyright © 2004 by Jacqueline Schiff. All rights reserved.

Keisha McDonnough for "You Are Not Alone." Copyright © 2004 by Keisha McDonnough. All rights reserved.

Barbara Cage for "Don't Give Up!" Copyright © 2004 by Barbara Cage. All rights reserved.

A careful effort has been made to trace the ownership of selections used in this anthology in order to obtain permission to reprint copyrighted material and give proper credit to the copyright owners. If any error or omission has occurred, it is completely inadvertent, and we would like to make corrections in future editions provided that written notification is made to the publisher:

BLUE MOUNTAIN ARTS, INC., P.O. Box 4549, Boulder, Colorado 80306.